Adventures in Canadian History

KINGS OF THE KLONDIKE

Books for Younger Readers by Pierre Berton

The Golden Trail
The Secret World of Og

ADVENTURES IN CANADIAN HISTORY
The Capture of Detroit
The Death of Isaac Brock
Revenge of the Tribes
Canada Under Siege

Bonanza Gold
The Klondike Stampede
Trails of '98
City of Gold
Before the Gold Rush
Kings of the Klondike

Parry of the Arctic
Jane Franklin's Obsession
Dr. Kane of the Arctic Seas
Trapped in the Arctic

The Railway Pathfinders
The Men in Sheepskin Coats
A Prairie Nightmare
Steel Across the Plains

PIERRE BERTON

KINGS OF THE KLONDIKE

ILLUSTRATIONS BY PAUL MC CUSKER

M&S

An M&S Paperback Original from
McClelland & Stewart Inc.
The Canadian Publishers

An M&S Paperback Original from McClelland & Stewart Inc.

First printing October 1993

Canadian Cataloguing in Publication Data

Berton, Pierre, 1920-
Kings of the Klondike

(Adventures in Canadian history. The great Klondike gold rush)
"An M&S paperback original."
Includes index.
ISBN 0-7710-1448-1

1. Millionaires – Yukon Territory – Biography – Juvenile literature.   2. Gold miners – Yukon Territory – Biography – Juvenile literature.   3. Klondike River Valley (Yukon) – Gold discoveries – Juvenile literature.   I. McCusker, Paul. II. Title. III. Series: Berton, Pierre, 1920-   . Adventures in Canadian history. The great Klondike gold rush.

FC4022.3.B47 1993   j971.9'102'0922   C93-094850-5
F1093.B47 1993

Series design by Tania Craan
Cover and text design by Stephen Kenny
Cover illustration by Scott Cameron
Interior illustrations by Paul McCusker
Maps by James Loates
Editor: Peter Carver

Typesetting by M&S

The support of the Government of Ontario through the Ministry of Culture, Tourism and Recreation is acknowledged

Printed and bound in Canada

McClelland & Stewart Inc.
The Canadian Publishers
481 University Avenue
Toronto, Ontario
M5G 2E9

Contents

Map appears on page 8

The events in this book actually happened as told here. Nothing has been made up. This is a work of non-fiction and there is archival evidence for every story and, indeed, every remark made in this book.

Adventures in Canadian History

KINGS OF THE KLONDIKE

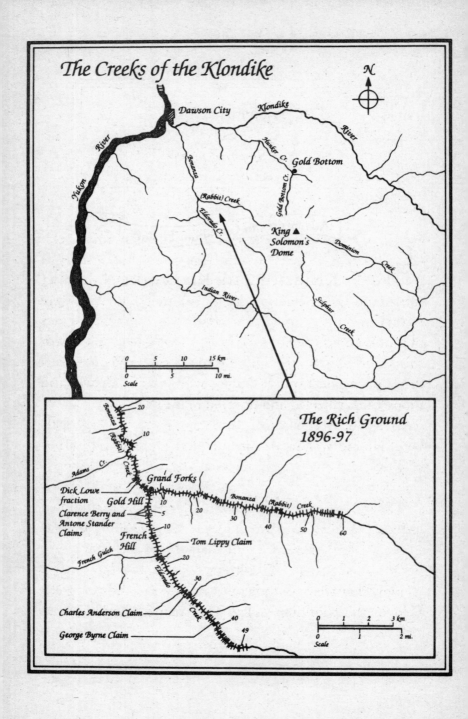

The Creeks of the Klondike

N

Dawson City

Klondike

River

Yukon

River

Bonanza

(Rabbit) Creek

Hunker Cr.

Gold Bottom

Gold Bottom Cr.

Eldorado Cr.

King
Solomon's
Dome ▲

Dominion

Creek

Indian River

Sulphur

Creek

0   5   10   15 km
0   5   10 mi.
Scale

The Rich Ground
1896-97

20

Bonanza

10

(Rabbit)

Creek

Adams Cr.

Grand Forks

Dick Lowe
fraction

Gold Hill

10

5
10

20

30

Bonanza

(Rabbit)   Creek

40

50

60

Clarence Berry and
Antone Stander
Claims

French
Hill

French Gulch

Tom Lippy Claim

20

Eldorado

30

Charles Anderson Claim

40

George Byrne Claim

49

Creek

0   1   2   3 km
0   1   2 mi.
Scale

CHAPTER ONE

~

Suitcases full of gold

THOMAS LIPPY SAT ON THE DECK of the stern-wheeler *Portus B. Weare,* contemplating the Yukon scenery as it rolled slowly past. It was late June, 1897, and the brief sub-Arctic spring had yielded to summer. The hills were aflame with drifts of crimson fireweed, set off by the blues of lupins and the yellows of daisies. The air was thick with the scent of the balm of Gilead poplar. Woodpeckers drummed against spruce trunks, while chicken hawks and moosebirds wheeled and hovered in the sky.

Life had been hard for Tom Lippy and his wiry little wife, Salome, who sat beside him on the foredeck. But they both knew that everything was about to change dramatically for the better.

The previous fall they had struck it rich on an unknown creek, now called Eldorado. Eldorado flowed into Bonanza Creek where the first gold strike had been made a few weeks before on August 16. But Eldorado was richer.

Now they were heading out with news of the new gold-field in the Klondike valley. That name, Klondike, was totally unknown. But soon it would be on everybody's lips, and Lippy and his fellow passengers would be known as the Kings of Eldorado or, more often, Kings of the Klondike.

The *Weare* and a second steamboat, *Alice,* were heading for civilization, each loaded with a single cargo: gold. There was gold in suitcases and leather grips, gold in boxes and packing cases, gold in belts and pokes of caribou hide, gold in jam jars, medicine bottles, and tomato cans, and gold in blankets held by straps and cords, so heavy it took two men to hoist each one aboard.

There was a total of more than three tons (2,722 kg) of gold on the two little steamboats. So heavy was the treasure that, on the three-storied *Weare,* the decks had to be shored up with wooden props.

Most of the eighty-odd passengers aboard the two vessels had been paupers a few months before. Now they were rich beyond their wildest dreams. Some had not seen civilization for years. None had heard from their families since the previous summer. One man, imprisoned in the Yukon for two years and reduced to a diet of half-raw salmon, had been planning suicide when he heard of the big strike in the Klondike. Now he was headed for civilization with thirty-five thousand dollars.

In 1897 that was an enormous fortune. You could rent a four-room apartment for a dollar and a quarter a week. You could buy an all-wool serge suit for four dollars. A three-course meal in a fancy restaurant cost twenty-five cents. Coffee was thirteen cents a pound. A nickel would buy two big baskets of tomatoes. But labourers made as little as a dollar for a ten-hour day. So the interest on thirty-five thousand would keep a man in relative luxury for the rest of his life.

Tom Lippy had a great deal more. He was worth at least one million dollars and his name would soon be on the lips of every literate American. He had started life as an iron moulder in Pennsylvania, but an almost fanatical belief in physical culture had led him into the YMCA and then on to Seattle as a physical training instructor.

As a volunteer fireman, Tom Lippy had once held the title of world's champion hose coupler and, like everyone else who had come in over the trail, he was tough, solidly built, dark, and clean-shaven. An injury to his knee had forced him to retire from the YMCA. A strange hunch had sent him north in 1896 on borrowed money. The hunch paid off. Now he had one of the richest claims in the Klondike.

At the old Russian port of St. Michael, near the Yukon's mouth, seventeen hundred miles (2,720 km) downriver from Dawson City at the mouth of the Klondike River, Lippy and his wife left their cramped quarters and switched to the ocean-going steamer *Excelsior*. A second ship, the *Portland*, was also waiting to take the overflow out to civilization.

These two grubby little vessels would bring the first detailed news of the great strike on Bonanza Creek to a waiting world. The Klondike valley was so remote from

Thomas Lippy and his wife aboard the Portus B. Weare.

civilization that it had no telegraph or telephone links with the outside world. That's why it took eleven months for the news of the gold strike to get out.

However, rumours of something big had been trickling down the Alaska Panhandle for some weeks. Had gold been discovered in huge quantities somewhere beyond the mists of the North? No one could be sure until the *Excelsior* arrived.

On July 17, 1897, the word was finally out. It came in the most dramatic fashion. Down the *Excelsior*'s gangplank and onto the wharf at San Francisco came the Klondike Kings, literally staggering under their loads of gold.

Here was Tom Lippy and his wife, grappling with a bulging suitcase weighing more than two hundred pounds (90 kg) – all gold. Here were Lippy's neighbours on Eldorado Creek: Frank Keller, a former railway brakeman, and his partner, Jim Clements, who had almost starved to death the previous year. Between them they had eighty-five thousand dollars in gold.

And here was one grizzled miner, fresh off the boat, ordering poached eggs, nine at a time, in a nearby restaurant, tipping the waitresses with nuggets, and hiring a horse-drawn cab to drive him around for twenty dollars a day. He had once pulled a hand sled for fourteen hundred miles (2,240 km), he told the crowd. Now he intended to ride in luxury.

In Seattle, the excitement was mounting because Lippy

was a local boy. He and his wife took a suite in San Francisco's Palace Hotel, where they found themselves virtual prisoners, the halls outside jammed with people bombarding the doors.

The *Portland* was due in Seattle at any moment. The daily newspaper, the *Post-Intelligencer,* sent a tugboat full of reporters out to intercept her. They tumbled over the ship's rails and into the arms of excited miners who were just as eager for news of the outside world as the newspapermen were of the Klondike strike.

The tug raced back to the city. By the time the *Portland* reached the dock, the paper had rushed three editions off its presses.

"GOLD! GOLD! GOLD!" the headlines read. "68 rich men on the steamer *Portland.* STACKS OF YELLOW METAL."

Five thousand people jammed Schwabacker's Dock at 6:00 a.m. on July 17 to watch the vessel arrive, and here the scenes at San Francisco were repeated.

John Wilkinson, a coal miner from Nanaimo, who had staked on Eldorado next door to Lippy, had fifty thousand dollars in gold in his leather grip. Although it was tied tightly with three straps, it was so heavy the handle snapped off as he staggered along the dock. Another, who had one hundred thousand dollars' worth of gold dust and nuggets tied up in a blanket, had to hire two helpers on the spot to help him drag it away.

Nils Anderson hoisted one heavy bag down the gangplank and then returned to his stateroom where he had two more sacks of gold. Two years before, he had borrowed three hundred dollars and left his family to gamble on fortune in the North. His wife, waiting on the docks, didn't know he was rich until he told her he had brought out one hundred and twenty thousand dollars' worth of gold.

Staff Sergeant M.E. Hayne of the North West Mounted Police, who had staked on Bonanza, came down the gangplank and into the arms of newsmen who "clung to us like limpets."

"Let me at least have a thimbleful of Scotch whisky before I suffer the torment of an interview," Hayne cried. Six men seized him and propelled him into a nearby saloon where each flung a quarter on the bar to treat him.

As the police struggled to hold back the crowds, every prospector found himself corralled by newsmen. Dick McNulty, who had twenty thousand dollars, announced that Klondike placer mining was ten times as rich as California. William Stanley, grey-haired and lame, announced that "the Klondike is no doubt the best place to make money that there is in the world."

Stanley's story was quickly circulated. A bookseller in Seattle, he had made and lost three fortunes in Rocky Mountain stampedes. Fifteen months earlier he had gone north with one son, Sam, on borrowed money and was ready to give up when an Indian drifted past his camp on the Yukon and said that white men had found much gold farther down the river.

Stanley now had one hundred and twenty thousand

dollars in gold. During his absence his wife had been living on wild berries and taking in laundry to keep her six children together. When the news reached her, she told her customers to fish their own things out of the tub, moved with her husband into a downtown hotel, threw out all her clothes, and called in a dressmaker to design garments suitable for the wife of a Klondike King.

From this day on, few of the Klondike Kings knew any real peace. The Stanleys were trailed by such crowds they had to flee to San Francisco. There, an avalanche of letters snowed them under. Clarence Berry, a former Circle City bartender, who had dug up a fortune on Eldorado, was tracked down to his hotel room by reporters. "The Klondike is the richest gold-field in the world," Berry declared. The newsmen goggled at four sacks of nuggets on the floor and a variety of jars and bottles on the table, all filled with gold.

Jacob Wiseman tried to get home to Walla Walla, Washington, but the mob that pressed upon him was so insistent he left town secretly to live under an assumed name in Tacoma.

Mrs. Eli Gage, daughter-in-law of the U.S. Secretary of the Treasury, whose husband's company owned the *Weare*, fled to the train station, boarded the train for Chicago, and locked herself in her drawing room for the entire journey.

Frank Phiscator, one of the original stakers on Eldorado, also headed for Chicago, flourishing a big red pocketbook containing a bank draft worth one hundred and twenty

Clarence Berry displays his wealth to reporters.

thousand dollars. When he checked into the Great Northern Hotel he told the clerk in ringing tones that nothing was too good for him.

After spending thirteen hard years trading along the Yukon, Joseph Ladue found himself eagerly accepted by his sweetheart's parents, who had once rejected him as a ne'er-do-well, but were now happy to welcome him into the family.

After all, Ladue had laid out the new town at the mouth of the Klondike and the papers were calling him the mayor of Dawson City. He was reputed to be worth five million dollars, a figure that established him securely as a man of financial genius. His picture appeared in advertisements endorsing such products as Dr. Green's Nervura blood and nerve remedy. His name appeared as the author of a book about the Klondike, and he was named president of a mining company whose directors included some of the biggest names in New York finance.

Ladue had spent his life searching for treasure from Wyoming to New Mexico to Arizona, and on to Alaska. He had begun as a youth operating a steam engine in a mine in the Black Hills. Now, suddenly, he found himself hobnobbing with merchant princes.

It did not last. Thirteen years of trading along the Yukon had taken their toll. Within a year Joseph Ladue was dead of tuberculosis at the very height of the great stampede that he had helped touch off.

CHAPTER TWO

Poor man's gold

B<small>Y THE END OF JULY THE WORD</small> "Klondike" instantly conjured up visions of sudden wealth. Thousands were fighting for steamship tickets to take them up the Alaska coast to the passes that led to the Yukon. (See *The Klondike Stampede* in this series.) Nobody was quite sure yet where the Klondike was; some believed it to be in Alaska and did not realize that they would have to pay customs duties and obey British law when they crossed into the Canadian Yukon.

It was a time for myth and legend – reinforced by interviews with the Klondike Kings, many of whom had made a habit of telling tall stories around the glowing stoves in their primitive log cabins.

In fact, the real stories were as remarkable as the false ones. Frank Phiscator, a Michigan farm boy, had worked his way west the previous year, carrying the mail on horseback to earn enough money to go north. He was one of a group of five who had trudged up the little creek that soon became known as Eldorado. Phiscator and his friends were now potential millionaires, for they had staked claims on the richest part of the creek, not far from its junction with the famous Bonanza. But like many others, Phiscator had no faith in his find. He sold half of his claim for eight hundred dollars, only to buy it back a few months later for fifteen thousand when the richness of Eldorado was proven.

Most of those who fought for steamboat tickets in the mad rush to the North had no idea how claims were staked in Canada or how placer gold was mined. Many believed it was lying in piles on the surface of the earth. Some of these gullible people thought they could shovel up the gold as easily as gravel. Indeed, they had brought along gunny sacks to hold their treasure!

After all, hadn't Tom Lippy of the Seattle YMCA, a man who knew nothing about mining, come out with a fortune? If Lippy could do it, anybody could!

Lippy's story was widely circulated. He had given up his job the previous spring on a hunch and headed north with his wife. He staked a claim high up on Eldorado but wasn't satisfied with it. Because his wife was with him, Lippy wanted to live in a cabin and so decided to move farther down the creek where there was more timber.

About a mile and a half (2.4 km) from the mouth of Eldorado, Lippy ran into four coal miners from Nanaimo, British Columbia, who had staked four claims – *Fourteen, Fifteen, Sixteen,* and *Seventeen.* The four Scotsmen – three brothers named Scouse and their partner, John Wilkinson

– didn't want to bet everything they had on a single package of ground and so abandoned two of their claims.

Lippy immediately re-staked Claim Number *Sixteen*. It proved to be the richest in the Klondike. Eventually it produced for him 1,530,000 dollars.

The Scouse brothers had also rejected *Seventeen*, next door to Lippy's ground. A prospector known as French Joe staked it, but having less faith than Lippy, sold it almost immediately for six hundred dollars. The buyer, Arkansas Jim Hall, an experienced prospector who had been ten years in the Yukon searching for gold, knew that at last he had found what he was seeking.

This claim, as it turned out, had the widest pay-streak in the country. When Jim Hall discovered what French Joe had given up he felt sorry for him, and he gave him seventy-five feet of the ground as a consolation prize.

Other stories whetted the appetites of the would-be gold-seekers. In the Klondike in the early months, poor men had become rich and then poor again without realizing it, as claims changed hands in the days following the big strike. Jay Whipple had staked at the very point where Eldorado flows into Bonanza – Claim Number *One*. He sold it for a trifle and later wished he hadn't. Skiff Mitchell, a lumberman from California, bought it. He lived for half a century on the proceeds.

Others hung on. Charles Lamb, who had been fired from his job as a Los Angeles streetcar conductor, refused to give up on his Number *Eight*. He and his partner finally sold it for three hundred and fifty thousand dollars. George Demars sold half of *Nine* for a mere eight hundred dollars. It was soon valued at a million.

A Chicago newspaperman, William Johns, who had been on the spot when Eldorado was discovered, sold half his Claim *Twelve* for five hundred dollars and thought himself lucky to get rid of it. Three months later he sold the other half for twenty-five hundred. It turned out to be one of the richest claims on the creek.

No wonder people talked of "Poor man's gold" and beggared themselves in order to join the mad race to the Yukon. (See *Trails of '98* in this series.)

All the gold in the Klondike was placer gold – "free gold," as the prospectors called it. Any man with a strong back, a shovel, and a pick could find it. It was not necessary to drill into the sides of mountains, or blast through ancient rock to reach a vein, for there were no veins of gold in the Klondike. These had long since been ground to dust and nuggets by wind and water through a natural sandpapering process that lasted millions of years.

The gold that bubbled up, molten, from the bowels of the earth was ground into smaller and smaller pieces, which were deposited in the bedrock of ancient streambeds. This wriggling line of gold was known as the "pay-streak." It followed the course of a prehistoric creek, now buried deep beneath a blanket of clay, muck, moss, and shrubbery through which a modern creek flowed.

Few of the would-be prospectors, all agog with tales of sudden riches, realized this. Nor did they realize that to seek and find the elusive pay-streak required backbreaking toil and a fair amount of luck. Claim owners had to burn a shaft ten, twenty, even thirty feet (3, 6, 9 m) down, setting fires at night, raking away the thawed earth in the morning, and building another fire to melt the next section of ground.

There were some advantages to mining in the North. No man needed to go to the trouble and expense of sawing wood to build a framework to prevent the shaft from falling in. The sides were permanently frozen, as hard as granite. A poor man's gold-field indeed!

But where was the pay-streak? It did not follow the course of the modern creek, which meant that a man might sink two or three shafts before finding it. Sometimes he would have to tunnel from the bottom of the shaft seeking the glittering trail of nuggets and dust – if indeed such a trail existed.

For this was the gamble. Few – certainly none of the amateurs – knew that the bulk of the gold lay in one section of the creek only. The claims near the upper end of Eldorado and Bonanza were empty of gold because the slopes were too steep. The force of rushing water had moved all the gold farther down. When the grade decreased, the larger nuggets began to sink beneath the water, to be caught in the grooves of the bedrock in the streambed.

The heaviest gold – and the richest – was thus deposited

first. Farther downstream, where the strength of the old currents weakened, finer gold was deposited. This explains why Tom Lippy's original claim, high up on Bonanza, was worthless, while the one he acquired from the Scottish miners – Number *Sixteen* – was fabulously rich.

At first no one had any idea how rich these claims were. Men had found a few nuggets on the surface, usually on the rim of the creekbeds; but until somebody burned his way down to bedrock to find the pay-streak, the Klondike was a gamble. A few determined men decided to do just that; and the four Nanaimo coal miners were among them.

The Scouse brothers decided to work *Fifteen,* one of the two claims they had retained. Bill Scouse was on the windlass and his brother Jack was down in the shaft, hoisting up heavy buckets of gravel, sand, and clay. Suddenly one bucket appeared whose contents were quite different from the others. Nuggets stuck out of the gravel like raisins in a cake, and fine gold glistened everywhere.

"What in hell do you think you sent up, the Bank of England?" Bill Scouse called down the shaft.

"What's up – have we struck it?" came the faint reply.

"Come up and have a look; it will do your blooming eyes good."

The two men sprinkled sand over the two pans of pay dirt to hide what they'd found. Then they went to their cabin and asked the third brother to pan out the gold. When he saw the result he thought he'd gone crazy. In those two pans was gold worth more than four hundred dollars – at twelve dollars an ounce.

Two industrious men had also sunk shafts to bedrock and found good pay. On *Twenty-one Above* Bonanza (where claims were numbered up- and downstream from the original discovery), Louis Rhodes hit the pay-streak on his first try. At the same time, Clarence Berry, a bartender from Fortymile, sank his pan in the crumbling bedrock at the base of his first shaft. From that single pan he weighed out fifty-seven dollars' worth of gold. Small wonder that his name was on everybody's lips and his story was being told and retold. (See *Bonanza Gold* in this series.)

These three finds proved the Klondike to be one of the richest mining areas in the world. It was not rich in the total quantity of gold it turned out, but certainly rich in the wealth of some of the individual claims. Until this time, ten-cent pans were considered good pay. Before the season was out, some men would be getting as much as eight hundred dollars from a single pan of selected pay dirt.

Most of the greenhorns who heard these tales after the treasure ships docked believed that even if you couldn't shovel gold into sacks, you could certainly pan it out of the creeks by hand. They didn't realize that once the pay-streak was found and the dirt hauled up into a "dump," as it was called, more backbreaking labour followed.

Mining in the Yukon was done in the winter. In the spring, when the snow melted and the hills were a-gurgle with rushing streams, the miners built long sluiceboxes and directed the water through them. Day after day they shovelled the gravel and muck from the dump into the boxes, where it was caught in cross bars and cocoa matting – just as it had once been caught in the coarse bedrock of the old stream beds. Every few days the water was redirected, the matting taken up, and the gold panned out.

No wonder, then, that many claim holders, unsure that they had any gold at all, let their claims lapse or sold them for a song, as Russian John Zarnowksy did. Zarnowsky owned Claim Number *Thirty* on Eldorado. He thought so little of it that he sold half of it to a big, lumbering Nova Scotian from Antigonish named Alex McDonald for a side of bacon and a sack of flour. There was very little gold above this claim, but Number *Thirty* turned out to be fabulously rich – so rich that Big Alex, as he was known, became the wealthiest man in the North, known to everyone as *the* King of the Klondike.

CHAPTER THREE

~

A story for Jack London

ALL OVER NORTH AMERICA AND AS FAR away as Europe and Australia, prospective millionaires, hoping to follow in Big Alex McDonald's footsteps, were studying placer mining law. Entire books rolled off the presses explaining the rules and retelling stories of sudden riches and missed opportunities.

A mining claim, they learned, was five hundred feet (152 m) long, stretching across the creek from rimrock to rimrock. Each claim had to be "located" by planting at each corner a four-foot (1.2 m) stake, known officially as a Mining Location Post, marked with the date, the number of the claim, and the name of the person making the claim.

Each prospector had sixty days to record his discovery at the mining recorder's office in the North West Mounted Police post at Fortymile, downriver near the Alaska border.

But in those early days few believed there was gold on either Eldorado or Bonanza. Many men staked claims in August and September 1896, and then left the area without bothering to record them. These unrecorded claims fell open in October and late November, and when that deadline arrived a wild scramble followed. By this time those on the ground realized how rich the Klondike was.

The most memorable incident had taken place on Upper Bonanza. Jack London, then on the verge of a spectacular career as a popular novelist, heard about it even before he reached the Klondike. Later, he used it in one of his Yukon stories.

The scene was a bizarre one. An unrecorded claim was

The Swede and the Scot race to file their claim.

about to fall open, and more than a dozen men milled about waiting for the midnight hour, intent on re-staking it. So tense was the situation that Mounted Police were stationed there to prevent trouble.

As the deadline approached, the contestants began to give up one by one, until only two were left – a Scotsman and a Swede. Both men had prepared their stakes in advance. Now they moved stubbornly to a starting line where, on the stroke of midnight, a policeman called "time"

and the race began. The two men hammered in their stakes and dashed off desperately down Bonanza Creek, neck and neck, heading for the mining recorder's office – some fifty miles downriver.

The two rivals, driving fast dog-teams, sped out onto the frozen Yukon, each realizing that the recorder's office closed at four in the afternoon and did not reopen until nine the next morning. Over the humpy ice they slid and tumbled, passing and repassing one another, until hours later, the blurred outline of the log town loomed out of the cold fog.

At this point the Scotsman's dogs began to flag. He leaped from his sled, determined to finish on foot. The Swede instantly followed suit. The two men reached the barrack gate in a dead heat.

The Swede, however, was unfamiliar with Fortymile. He raced for the largest building, but that turned out to be quarters for the NWMP officers. The Scot, knowing the layout, let him go, made a sharp turn to the right, and just managed to reach the door of the recording office. He was too exhausted to cross the six-inch threshold. He fell on it, crying with his remaining strength, "*Sixty Above* on Bonanza!" An instant later the Swede toppled across him, gasping out the same phrase.

The police advised the pair to divide the ground, which in the end they did. As it turned out, the disputed claim, being too high up the valley, was entirely worthless.

There were plenty of similar stories going the rounds.

But the most unbelievable ones weren't fiction – they were true, like the tale of the Dick Lowe Fraction.

Dick Lowe, a rugged, wiry man, had been a muleskinner in Idaho. He had already made and lost a fortune in the Black Hills of that state and was now in the Yukon, hoping to recoup his losses.

Lowe went to work on Bonanza, not for a wealthy prospector, but for William Ogilvie, a Canadian government surveyor who had been asked by the miners to straighten out the mess on Bonanza Creek. Many claims had been badly measured by the early stakers, and Ogilvie discovered that several were too big. To restore these claims to the regulation five hundred feet, a fractional piece was cut from them. These little pieces of ground were now open for re-staking.

Nobody knew it, but the richest fraction of all lay on Bonanza Creek just above George Carmack's discovery. Here, almost at the junction of Bonanza, Eldorado, and Big Skookum Gulch, a prospector had staked *Two Above*. But he had bitten off too much land, and when Ogilvie measured the claim he found a small wedge, only eighty-six feet (26 m) at its broadest point, left over.

Dick Lowe stared at the sliver of land.

"Had you thought of staking it?" he asked Ogilvie.

"I'm a government official and not permitted to hold property," the surveyor replied. "You go down if you like and record."

Lowe didn't know what to do. It was a very small piece of ground. If he staked, he wouldn't be able stake another claim on Bonanza – a bigger one, he hoped. On the other hand he had come very late to the Klondike and there wasn't much left to stake.

Lowe decided to take a chance, but before staking the fraction on Bonanza, he decided to look for a larger piece. He could find nothing. The little wedge of property did not excite him. He tried to sell it for nine hundred dollars. Nobody would buy it. He tried to lease it, but again there were no takers. The claim was just too small. In the end he decided to work it himself.

Dick Lowe sank a shaft and found nothing. He sank another and – *Eureka!* – in eight hours he cleaned up forty-six thousand dollars in gold. The Dick Lowe Fraction, as it came to be called, eventually paid out half a million dollars. It remains, for its size, the richest single piece of ground ever discovered.

It could have been Ogilvie's, but in that incorruptible surveyor's letters and articles, pamphlets and memoirs, there is no hint of regret. Indeed, it's doubtful that the possibility of wealth ever crossed his mind. As far as Ogilvie was concerned, the gold might as well have been on the moon.

This fraction was situated in the most promising spot in the whole district. Two of the richest creeks, Bonanza and Eldorado, met here, pouring down their gold onto the property. A third stream, Big Skookum Gulch, cut directly through another ancient gold-bearing channel, whose presence was still unknown. Just above stood Gold Hill, still unnamed, still unstaked, but heavy with coarse gold, much of it washing down onto the property below.

Lowe's ground was so rich that a wire had to be strung along the border of his claim to prevent trespassers. Whenever a nugget was found along the boundary line, its ownership was determined by a plumb bob, which slid along this wire. In August 1899, a single pan of pay dirt scooped up from an adjoining claim a few feet below the fraction, yielded a thousand dollars in gold.

It was said that as much gold was stolen from Lowe's property as he himself recovered from it. In some places glittering nuggets were visible from a distance of twenty feet (6 m). Alas, like so many others, Lowe was never the same man again. Almost from the moment of discovery he got drunk and stayed that way.

Chapter Four

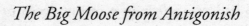

The Big Moose from Antigonish

By the time the first waves of the great stampede reached the Yukon, two of the most durable legends of the Klondike had begun to take form.

One was the legend of Big Alex McDonald, the King of the Klondike. The other was the legend of Swiftwater Bill Gates, the Knight of the Golden Omelet. None of the kings of Eldorado were destined for greater immortality than these two strange figures, so different from each other – the one a towering and sober Canadian, the other a pint-sized colourful Yankee.

Both acquired their fortunes because of the "lay system," which McDonald introduced to the Klondike. He had come to the North after fourteen years in the silver mines of Colorado and a stint in Juneau on the Alaska Panhandle. Although he had no money, he had developed a shrewd sense of values while working as a buyer of land for the Alaska Commercial Company. Now he had an abiding faith in the value of property that amounted almost to a religion.

While other men owned a single claim and worked it themselves, McDonald was determined to own a great many and let others do the work. He had begun by acquiring half of *Thirty* Eldorado from Russian John Zarnowsky for a few groceries. He made no move to mine it. Instead he let a section of it out on lease, or "lay," as it was called. The two men who leased it paid him a percentage of what they found. In the next forty-five days, the pair took out thirty-three thousand dollars in gold. McDonald got half.

With his purchase of Claim Number *Thirty* on Eldorado, McDonald began his climb from day labourer to Klondike King. Because of his size and his awkward movements, he was known as the Big Moose from Antigonish. He spoke slowly and painfully, rubbing his blue jowls in perplexity, his great brow almost hidden by a shock of black hair, his heavy lips concealed by a huge moustache. But behind those features was one of the shrewdest minds in the North.

While others sold, McDonald bought and continued to buy as long as there was breath in his body. Soon he was famous, renowned on three continents as the "King of the Klondike," and sought out by pope, prince, and promoter.

As fast as the lay men gave him his share, he bought more property. His policy was to make a small down payment and give a promissory note for the balance, payable at the time of the spring clean-up. To raise enough money for these down payments, he borrowed funds at heavy interest.

In some cases he paid as much as 10 per cent for a ten-day loan, which is a rate of 365 per cent per annum.

By late spring, Big Alex McDonald's speculations were the talk of the camp. Clean-up time was approaching. It was no longer possible to work in the drifts and shafts, which were filling with seepage from the melting snow and ice. The miners were building flumes and log sluiceboxes and paying a high price for rough lumber.

Everybody waited expectantly. Not until the gold was washed from the gravel of the winter dumps would anyone know exactly how much Big Alex was worth. Until this was done it was all mere guesswork.

Bets were laid as to whether he would be bankrupt or wealthy by summer. The people to whom he owed money were demanding payment. Often enough he had to pay them off with gold still wet from the sluiceboxes.

On one occasion fate stepped in to save him from ruin. He owed forty thousand dollars to two brothers. When the debt fell due, he still hadn't washed out enough gold to pay his debt. At the eleventh hour one of the brothers conveniently died. The lawsuit that followed delayed payments until McDonald was able to meet the loan.

Before the summer of '97 was out, McDonald had interests in twenty-eight claims, and his holdings were reckoned in millions of dollars. "I've invested my whole fortune," he remarked. "I've run up debts of one hundred and fifty thousand dollars besides. But I can dig out one hundred and fifty thousand any time I need it."

Nobody knew what he was worth – and that included Big Alex himself. It was said that if he so much as stopped to look at a piece of property, its value increased at once. He was involved in so many complicated business deals that every time he was introduced to a newcomer he would start out by asking, "Are you a partner of mine?"

Wherever he went, a swarm of hangers-on followed, plucking at his sleeve, waving papers, offering deals, asking for money. Big Alex always answered with an immediate "No!" But that only meant he wanted time to think over the scheme. As often as not he ended by accepting it, for he had reached the point where he found it hard to turn down any offer.

With his slow speech, his great hands, and his blank features, the King of the Klondike presented a simple face to the world. He rarely showed any emotion, but the deals he made were highly complex.

In June of 1897, he walked into the tent office of Ron Crawford, a former Seattle court clerk who was setting up in a business to draw up legal papers for prospectors. McDonald deposited his huge frame on the three-legged stool in front of Crawford's rough spruce table and announced he wanted to borrow five thousand dollars. Crawford, who had only twenty-five cents to his name, asked him how much interest he was willing to pay.

"I don't want to pay interest," said McDonald in his slow way, rubbing his chin. "Interest is always working against you, and I can't sleep at night when I think of that. But if you let me have the money, I'll give you a lay of one hundred feet (30 m) of *Six Below* Bonanza at 50 per cent. I'll also give you 35 per cent of thirty-five feet (11 m) of *Twenty-seven* Eldorado, and a mortgage on *Thirty* Eldorado as security."

Considering the value of these three claims, it was an enormous sum to pay for the use of five thousand dollars. Crawford stalled for time. He promised to give McDonald an answer by morning. Then he rushed to a neighbouring saloon and raised five thousand dollars from the owner in return for a half-interest in the mortgage on *Thirty*. After the loan was made, Crawford sold part of his share of the section of *Twenty-seven* for five thousand dollars to a Dawson barber. The barber worked it the following winter and took out forty thousand dollars. McDonald's example was widely copied. Claims were carved up like so many apple pies – mortgaged, leased, traded, loaned, lost.

George Carmack, the original discoverer of Bonanza, sold half of his brother-in-law's claim for five thousand dollars. The buyer put five hundred dollars down and went to work. From a fourteen-foot (4.3 m) shaft he immediately took out eight thousand, from which he paid off the balance. Ogilvie recognized that on this basis the claim could be worth about two and a half million.

"My God," cried the new owner, "what will I do with all that money?"

"I wouldn't worry," Ogilvie told him. "It's hardly

possible your claim will average anything like that." And he went on to reason that if the only wealth on the claim was on the one fourteen-foot strip, there would still be eighty-three thousand dollars in the ground. And that, he added dryly, "is enough to kill you."

Chapter Five

~

The legend of Swiftwater Bill

THE SYSTEM THAT MADE Big Alex McDonald rich catapulted Swiftwater Bill Gates into the notoriety he wanted so badly. Gates was one of a group of seven men who were finally persuaded to take the lay on *Thirteen* Eldorado, which had been shunned by everybody else because of the jinx of the number thirteen. The new men sank seven shafts before they hit pay dirt. When they did they saw at once it was incredibly rich.

They wanted to keep it a secret, so they burned in the sides of the shaft and let it be noised about that they were getting a paltry ten cents to the pan. The owner, J.B. Hollingshead, was delighted that April to sell them the property for forty-five thousand dollars. In just six weeks they were able to pay him with gold dug out of his own claim.

Until this point there was little to distinguish William F. Gates from his fellows. He was only five-foot-five (1.7 m), and his moon face was ornamented by a straggling black moustache that gave his features a comic look. No one ever took him seriously. When he boasted of his former powers as a boatman on a river in Idaho they laughed and gave him the nickname "Swiftwater Bill."

Like most of his companions, Swiftwater Bill Gates was nearly broke. But all he needed to transform his personality was gold. In 1896 he had been working as a nondescript dishwasher. By 1897 he was a man in a Prince Albert coat, with a top hat, a white shirt, a diamond stickpin in his tie, and the only starched collar in Dawson. It was said that he was so proud of his unique collar that he took to his bed while it was being laundered, rather than be seen without it.

All his life Bill Gates had been a small man – a face in the crowd with nothing to set him aside from his fellows. Now he decided to be Somebody.

He didn't wait for his share of the gold to be hauled up the shaft of *Thirteen* Eldorado. He borrowed money at 10 per cent a month so he could play pool at a hundred dollars a frame, or throw his poke on the faro table and cry, "The sky's the limit! Raise her up as far as you want to go, boys, and if the roof's in the way, why, tear it off."

One night Swiftwater lost five hundred dollars in a few minutes. "Things don't seem to be coming my way tonight," he said, rising from his seat. "Let's let the house have a drink at my expense." That cost him 112 dollars. In spite of his losses he threw the rest of his poke on the bar, lighted a dollar-fifty cigar, and strolled out.

Like Big Alex, he hired others to do his mining for him. But whereas Big Alex used all his time to acquire more gold,

Swiftwater used every waking moment to get rid of his. Like Big Alex, he paid his workers in property rather than in cash, and he paid them well.

One of his helpers, a former milk-wagon driver from Seattle named Harry Winter, worked a hundred days for Swiftwater and received in return a fifty-foot-square (15.2 m) plot of ground. From that he took five thousand dollars, which he used to buy from Swiftwater a second plot thirty-feet square (9 m). That yielded eighty-five thousand. It meant that Swiftwater had, in effect, paid Winter nine hundred dollars a day for his labour.

Swiftwater Bill allowed no wine to touch his lips (though he occasionally bathed in it), but he indulged in other pleasures. It was his habit to escort dance-hall girls to his claim and let them clamber down the shaft to pan out all the gold they wanted. They turned out to be as expert as seasoned miners.

Bill's favourite was Gussie Lamore, a nineteen-year-old who had come to Dawson from Circle City in the spring rush and who shared top billing with him in an incident that has become the liveliest of the Klondike's imperishable legends.

Gussie, it turned out, was very fond of fresh eggs, possibly because they were as scarce as diamonds in the Dawson of 1897. One day, so the tale goes, Swiftwater Bill was seated in a restaurant when, to his surprise and chagrin, he saw Gussie enter on the arm of a well-known gambler. The pair ordered fried eggs, which were the most expensive item on the menu, and it was then that, in a fury of jealousy, Swiftwater achieved a certain immortality by buying up every egg in town in an attempt to frustrate Gussie's cravings.

They called him the "Knight of the Golden Omelet." There are many versions of this tale. Arthur Walden, a dog driver, who claimed in his memoirs to have witnessed the incident, wrote that Swiftwater had the eggs fried one at a time and then flipped them through the window of the café to a rabble of dogs outside, commenting to the gathering crowd on the cleverness of the animals in catching them.

Other versions have it that he presented the entire treasure of eggs to Gussie as a token of his true emotions, or that he fed them to other dance-hall girls in order to awaken Gussie's jealousy. Belinda Mulroney, a famous Klondike innkeeper who arrived in Dawson early that spring, recollects that there was about half a case of eggs involved, and that these had been brought over the ice from the Pacific coast and were fast growing mellow. Mrs. Iola Beebe, one of Swiftwater's several future mothers-in-law, wrote that there were two crates of eggs and that Swiftwater paid for them with two coffee tins filled with gold.

The details of the story have thus been lost, for there was no writing-paper in Dawson at the time to set them down, and no writers either, since every would-be historian was too busy seeking a fortune to attend to such footnotes. Whatever the details, the fact remains that the incident won Gussie over, at least temporarily. She offered to meet

Swiftwater Bill in San Francisco that fall and marry him, failing to mention that she was already wed to one Emile Leglice, and had been since 1894.

Swiftwater's journey to San Francisco was supposed to be for business. He had gone into partnership with a clever businessman named Jack Smith to establish the most famous of the Klondike's palaces of pleasure, the Monte Carlo Dance Hall and Saloon.

Smith was an old showman who had a variety troupe in Fortymile at the time of the strike. He had reached Bonanza with the first wave, staked a claim, sold it for 155,000 dollars, opened up a small saloon on the creeks, and turned a handy profit. That convinced him that it was easier to dig gold out of the miners' pockets than out of the ground.

Smith saw that there were more riches to be mined on Dawson's Front Street than in the creeks of the Klondike Valley. He immediately opened the Monte Carlo in a tent. He made only one error of judgement, but it was a whopper. He persuaded Swiftwater Bill to put up some of the funds for a permanent building. Then he allowed him to go out to San Francisco to rustle up a cargo of furnishings, liquor, and dance-hall girls.

Sending Swiftwater Outside to bring back girls was like sending a greedy child to a candy shop and hoping to get a full box back. But the awful realization of what he had done did not begin to dawn on Jack Smith until the following summer.

When Swiftwater arrived in San Francisco, he rented a

suite of rooms in the Baldwin Hotel and in the Klondike manner began to distribute gold dust to everybody he met. He tipped the bellboys to walk about the lobby and point him out to hotel guests as the "King of the Klondike." Then he paid a journalist one hundred dollars to publish a lurid account of his own drowning.

In his new Prince Albert coat, and with diamond cuff links and diamond stickpin, he presented to the world a glittering figure, in spite of his small size and his scraggly moustache. Alas for Swiftwater, Gussie Lamore, who had gone ahead of him, refused to go through with her promise of marriage, possibly because in addition to being already married she had a three-year-old child.

Undaunted, Swiftwater then married her sister Grace, bought her a fifteen-thousand-dollar house, and while it was being fixed up to suit his taste, put her in the bridal chamber of the Baldwin. The honeymoon, however, was short-lived; Grace threw him over after three weeks. Still undaunted, Swiftwater began earnestly to woo the youngest Lamore sister, Nellie.

By this time he was running out of money and hadn't bought anything for Jack Smith's Monte Carlo. Swiftwater, however, was a born prospector. He was always able to spot a likely piece of ground and, where there was no ground available, to spot a likely looking sucker. His eye fell on a Dr. Wolf, who had twenty thousand dollars to invest. Swiftwater talked so swiftly and smoothly that he was able to get all of it. In return he gave Wolf a ninety-day note promising to pay the astonishing interest rate of 100 per cent.

But Wolf's imagination was so fired by Swiftwater's tale of fortunes in the Klondike that he decided to become a stampeder himself. The two laid plans to organize a trading and transportation company and set off at once for Seattle. There, the doctor plunged into the business end of the venture while Swiftwater paraded up and down the street with the girls he'd hired for the Monte Carlo Dance Hall.

He lived extravagantly at the Rainier-Grand Hotel, and ordered gallons of champagne, not to drink – for he was a teetotaller – but to bathe in! He splashed about in the tub for the benefit of the press, announcing that a bath was a rare thing in the Yukon. When he left, the bill for damages alone came to fifteen hundred dollars.

Dr. Wolf began to become suspicious. Slowly it dawned on him that his new partner was not the solid businessman he had thought he was. By the time they reached Lake Bennett, Wolf was thoroughly alarmed. He left Swiftwater behind and sped ahead to Dawson by dog-sled to investigate his new partner's background before the main rush arrived. The stories he heard of Swiftwater's escapades in the city of gold only confirmed his worst fears.

When Swiftwater reached Dawson, both Wolf and Jack Smith were waiting on the riverbank for him. It was, perhaps, the most exotic arrival in the Klondike's brief history. For there was Swiftwater, in the prow of a Peterborough canoe, with two scow-loads of girls and whisky towed

Swiftwater Bill Gates enjoys a champagne bath.

behind. With a silk top hat cocked on his head, and his Prince Albert coat draped across his shoulders, he extended his arms in a welcome to the crowd who stood on the bank to greet him. Directly behind him a girl was perched on a case of whisky, and on the scow other girls waved and shouted greetings to the onlookers.

Swiftwater stepped ashore in triumph – into the arms of his enraged partner.

"You've got just exactly three hours to pay back the twenty thousand," Wolf told him. "To hell with the interest!"

"I'll have it," Swiftwater gasped.

"Get started!" Wolf rapped back. Swiftwater raised the money. Wolf took the next boat home declaring he'd had all he wanted of the Klondike. Jack Smith lost no time in taking over twelve thousand dollars of Swiftwater's mining profit in the bank and Swiftwater's share of the dance hall as well.

But nothing fazed Swiftwater Bill Gates. With scarcely an instant's hesitation, he plunged into a new scheme, announcing the formation of a trading and exploration company. He left directly for London to raise the capital. He was not a man whose spirits were easily dampened.

CHAPTER SIX

The Klondike queen

PAT GALVIN OF BONANZA CREEK summed up the spirit of '98 in a few short sentences of advice given to his nephew who'd arrived from the Outside that summer. His nephew, watching the way Galvin flung away his money, tried to utter a few words of caution about expense.

"Expense! Expense!" cried Galvin. "I'm disgusted with you. Don't show your ignorance by using that cheap Outside word. We don't use it here. Never repeat it in my presence again. You must learn the ways of Alaska. That word is not understood in the north. If you have money, spend it; that's what it's for, and that's the way we do business."

That might easily have stood as the Klondike's creed in the year of the stampede. The gold that had lain hidden for so long in the frozen gravels now moved as swiftly as the nuggets Galvin gave away like souvenirs to any passing stranger.

The Kings of Bonanza and Eldorado who'd been common labourers two years before now saw themselves as captains of industry. They were determined to invest their new-found wealth. Some built hotels and fitted them out with Persian carpets and mahogany furniture. Others financed restaurants that served everything from oysters to sherbet. Dozens were sucked into mining companies, syndicates, trading firms, and transportation companies.

Galvin, a one-time town marshal in Helena, Montana, was now rich because of his Bonanza claim. He, too, started a transportation company. His reputation for free spending was well known. It was said he was good for two thousand dollars a night in Dawson. On entering a bar it was his custom to treat everybody in the house.

"Come on, boys," Galvin would shout. "Open up the best you have, the drinks are on me!" In case he might have overlooked anybody on the street, he would send the bartender outside to drag in any passerby. He was a commanding figure, dressed entirely in black, slender and wiry, with eyes that gleamed from a pale Irish face. A crowd usually followed him, for his generosity was legend and he distributed as much as a thousand dollars' worth of nuggets at a time.

Unable to give away all of his money, Galvin bought a steamboat, the *Yukoner*, for forty-five thousand dollars. Others followed his example, becoming, if only briefly, shipping magnates. Big Alex McDonald bought the *W.K. Merwyn* and also acquired the *W.F. Stratton*, named for an eccentric Black Hills mining millionaire.

Nels Peterson, who had grown rich from one of the early claims, formed the "Flyer" line with two spanking new steamboats, the *Eldorado* and the *Bonanza King*. The original name of the *Eldorado* was *Philip B. Low,* but she sank so many times that she was referred to as the "Fill Up Below," and so the name was changed.

Peterson offered a free ticket from Dawson to Seattle to the first person to spot either boat when the two arrived on their maiden voyage from St. Michael at the mouth of the Yukon in the fall of '98. Hundreds who had no other way of leaving the Klondike climbed to the Midnight Dome – the tall hill above the town – straining for the sight of steamboat smoke. One ingenious pair won handily by arranging a system of wig-wag signals from the mountaintop to friends on the main street. Dozens risked breaking their necks in a pell-mell race down the hillside when the *Bonanza King* at last appeared, only to find they'd been outwitted. But Peterson's showmanship was better than his business sense. He sank ninety thousand dollars in the two boats, and that helped to ruin him.

The Kings of the Klondike demanded every luxury. By the end of August, fifty-six steamboats had dumped seventy-four hundred tons (6,600 tonnes) of freight on the new docks – everything from fancy porcelain chamber pots to flagons of Napoleon brandy.

Dawson was no longer a beans and bacon town. The imported San Francisco chef at the Regina Hotel served Rock Point oysters, Lobster Newburg, grilled moose chops with mushrooms, roast beef, and Bengal Club chutney. Its floors were covered with Brussels carpets. Its woodwork had gold-leaf trimming. It rose four storeys, the tallest building in Dawson.

Its chief rival was the equally elegant Fairview, which Belinda Mulroney was constructing on Front Street. Belinda planned to make it the finest hotel in town. It was to have twenty-two steam-heated rooms, a side entrance for ladies, Turkish baths, and electric lights whose power would be supplied by a yacht anchored in the river.

The tables were spread with linen, sterling silver, and bone china. In the lobby an orchestra played chamber music. The bar was staffed by young American doctors and dentists who couldn't get a licence to practise on British soil but quickly learned to mix drinks instead of medicines.

Belinda is one of the most remarkable figures turned up by the Klondike gold stampede. She was a plain-faced young Irishwoman, rigid in her moral standards, but shrewder than most of the men who found sudden riches in the creeks of the Klondike.

She was born in Scranton, Pennsylvania, the daughter of a coal miner. When the great Columbian Exposition opened in Chicago in 1892 she went there to open a restaurant hoping to make her fortune. She was only eighteen at the time.

She earned eight thousand dollars in the restaurant business but lost it all in when she went out west to California. That didn't bother her. She shipped aboard the *City of Topeka* as a stewardess. There, she quickly gained a reputation for her business sense, her coolness, and the sharpness of her tongue. Once a passenger made the mistake of asking her to black his boots. She said that if he so much as put them outside his door, she would pour a pitcher of water on them.

On her voyage a baby had to be delivered. Belinda did the job herself, while the captain stood discreetly outside the cabin door, reading instructions from a medical book.

She was put in charge of purchasing all the ship's supplies, buying everything from machinery to canary birds. For that she charged the captain a stiff 10 per cent commission. When the ship stopped at the various coastal towns, Belinda was on hand to sell picture hats and satin dresses to the Indian women.

By the spring of 1897, when the first news of the Klondike strike reached the Alaska Panhandle, Belinda had saved five thousand dollars. She decided to invest it all in cotton goods and hot-water bottles. Down the Yukon River she went, on a raft piloted by two Indians. When she reached Dawson she took her last fifty-cent piece and threw it into the river, swearing she'd never again need such small change. And she was right.

In Dawson she sold her merchandise at a profit of 600 per cent. Then she opened up a lunch counter and hired a group of young men to build cabins for her. She sold those as fast as the roofs went on.

But Belinda wanted to be nearer to the gold and so she bought a broken-down mule named Gerry and began to haul timber out to the creeks. The town jeered, but Belinda went ahead building a roadhouse. Her friends told her that it was the wrong place – that the only place to open a hotel and a saloon was in Dawson itself. But they were wrong.

Belinda opened her inn in the fall of 1897 at the junction of Bonanza and Eldorado creeks. A wild little town was already springing up there, servicing those miners who didn't want to make the long trip into Dawson. It was called Grand Forks and the population reached five thousand. Belinda stood behind the bar, a stern figure in her white shirtwaist and long black skirt, selling eggs at a dollar apiece, and wine, cigars, and whisky at the highest prices in the Klondike. She was on her way to making her first fortune.

All this time she kept her ears open to the mining gossip. The Eldorado Kings flocked to her roadhouse. Belinda made a note of everything she heard. Before the winter was over, she had half a dozen valuable mining properties in her name.

She never missed an opportunity to make a profit. That fall a small boat loaded with supplies had been wrecked on a sand bar. Belinda immediately went into partnership with Big Alex McDonald to buy and salvage the cargo. McDonald moved quickly, grabbing all the food and leaving Belinda with nothing but several cases of rubber boots and whisky.

"You'll pay through the nose for this," Belinda vowed. She meant it. The following spring, when the land around the creeks was thick with mud, Big Alex arrived at her

Belinda Mulroney at her inn at Grand Forks.

roadhouse in a hurry, looking for rubber boots for his workers. She charged him a hundred dollars a pair.

Meanwhile she was planning her elegant hotel – the Fairview – on Dawson's Front Street. It opened in July of 1898, but more than a year was required to put the finishing touches to it.

All the Fairview's furnishings – from cut glass chandeliers to brass bedsteads – had to be packed in over the White Pass. Belinda, who left very little to others, went personally to Skagway to supervise that operation.

She arrived in the nick of time. Joe Brooks, the packer she had hired, had moved her outfit only two miles (3.2 km) up the trail. Then he dumped it when he received a better offer to transport a cargo of whisky for Bill McPhee's saloon.

Belinda became very angry. She headed for the Skagway wharves and recruited a gang of jobless men. She goaded them into fighting among themselves until she found out which one was the toughest. She elected him foreman, and, that done, she accompanied the gang up the trail to take over from Brooks.

Her men beat up Brooks's foreman, imprisoned him in a tent, set a guard outside of it, and dumped McPhee's whisky on the side of the trail. Then they loaded Belinda's hotel equipment on Brooks's mules, and started over the pass. Belinda, mounted on Brooks's own pinto pony, rode at the head of this odd procession. In this manner she got the entire shipment safely over the mountains and then down the Yukon River on fifteen scows.

Now the Fairview stood complete. It had only one real flaw. The interior walls were made of canvas, over which wallpaper had been pasted so that the slightest whisper anywhere in the building could be heard by every guest.

Thomas Cunningham, purser of the *Yukoner,* once invited Belinda to have breakfast with him at the hotel. She was delighted to accept. When the bill was added up, it came to sixty dollars. That was an enormous sum of money for breakfast at a time when workmen in the outside world were making between a dollar and two dollars a day. Cunningham certainly was staggered.

"Think of a woman ordering champagne for breakfast!" he exclaimed. "It is not done." But it was done in Dawson City in Belinda Mulroney's day.

By 1899 Belinda was one of the wealthiest and most powerful women in the Klondike. In spite of her prim ways and her plain Irish features she was a good catch for any enterprising bachelor. And such a man duly arrived on the scene. He sported a monocle, kid gloves, spats, a small, jet-black moustache, and a tall, bearded valet.

From an elegant leather case he produced an engraved calling card:

M. Le Comte Carbonneau
Représentant
Messieurs Pierre Legasse, Frères et Cie
Bordeaux   Paris   New York

He wasn't a count at all. He was a champagne salesman from Quebec. But he fell for Belinda. Every day he sent her a bunch of red roses at her hotel, and Belinda fell for him.

In October of 1900 the coal miner's daughter from Scranton became a countess. Her husband, of course, was a fraud. Tom Lippy's French-Canadian foreman, Joe Putraw, had positively identified him as a barber from Montreal's Rue Saint-Denis. Belinda didn't care.

Off the couple went to Paris, where they rode up and down the Champs-Élysées behind a pair of handsome snow-white horses decked out with a gold-ornamented harness. An Egyptian footman unrolled a velvet carpet of brilliant crimson whenever they stepped out.

Belinda herself continued to prosper in the Yukon. She became the only woman mining manager in the territory – and of the largest mining company. The Gold Run Mining Company had got into financial difficulties, largely because the owners spent all their profits at a gaming table they were running, while their employees stole gold off the property in order to gamble with it. The local bank manager put Belinda in charge. In just eighteen months the company was showing a profit.

Belinda's first move was to throw out the roulette wheel and replace it with a bridge table. Her second was to drive all women from the property. As a forewoman, she was a holy terror. One old sourdough retained vivid memories of working for her. He recalled that she wouldn't allow any smoking on the job. He tried to break this rule, but before he had a match lit she gave a low whistle, crooked her finger, and said sharply, "Get off this claim before nightfall." He did.

After the Klondike strike was over, Belinda and her husband went on to Fairbanks during the Tanana mining boom in Central Alaska. In 1910 they left the North at last and bought themselves a ranch near Yakima, Washington. There, in the style of so many of their fellows, they built themselves a stone castle.

Every winter they went to Europe, where Carbonneau became a bank director and a steamship magnate. They put all their money into the steamship company. But when World War One came, it brought an end to merchant shipping. Carbonneau was killed during the war and Belinda went back to Washington State, where she lived with her memories until her death in the early 1960s.

But long after the gold fever had died away, hundreds of Yukoners still remembered the plain-faced Irishwoman who dug so much gold, not out of the ground of Bonanza and Eldorado, but out of the pockets of those who had already found it.

CHAPTER SEVEN

The fate of kings

BY 1899, THE KINGS OF THE KLONDIKE had become a distinct social class. In the dance-halls they occupied the royal boxes high above the floor. They drove their fashionable dog-teams down the hard-packed snow of the Klondike valley in the same way that British aristocrats drove their Rolls Royces through the streets of London.

The dog-team had become a symbol. The Klondike Kings, the saloonkeepers, gamblers, and mine owners, all kept expensive teams with expensive harness. One man, "Coatless Curly" Munro, in a single season fed his puppies a total of 4,320 pounds (1,960 kg) of bacon, fish, and flour, at a dollar a pound, hoping they would grow up to be a prize team. Coatless Curly got his nickname because he never wore an overcoat, even in the coldest weather – though, it was said, he did have several layers of underwear.

Jim Daugherty had a prize team of eight dogs worth twenty-five hundred dollars and a sled which had its own built-in bar. That was a specially made tin tank he kept filled with alcohol, which he poured out by the dipperful to mix with hot water and sugar for his friends.

Waste, on a grand scale, went along with wealth on a grand scale. Dick Lowe, the man who had staked the famous fraction on Bonanza, could be seen on Sunday afternoons driving a spanking team of trotting horses along the Klondike valley with a dance-hall girl at his side – or in the evening flinging a fortune on the bars of Dawson's saloons to treat the entire crowd.

On Dominion Creek two neighbouring miners each installed a butler in his log cabin. On Eldorado, Clarence Berry enjoyed a peculiar luxury: he owned the only cow in the valley, a purebred Jersey, who supplied fresh milk from her sawdust-padded stable and munched hay worth four hundred dollars a ton (907 kg). In front of Berry's cabin, along the Eldorado trail, stood a coal-oil can full of gold and a bottle of whisky beside. A sign between the two of them carried the blunt but inviting message: "Help yourself."

Berry's partner, the handsome Antone Stander, who had staked the first of the Eldorado claims, went out to San Francisco with his new wife, a dance-hall girl named Violet Raymond. He planned to take her on a honeymoon to China, and he had a thousand pounds of gold as pocket money in his stateroom. Bit by bit he gave the gold to Violet; she spent it all.

Charley Anderson, known as the Lucky Swede because

he had bought a million-dollar claim while drunk, went off to Europe accompanied by his wife, the same Grace Drummond who had caught the eye of Swiftwater Bill Gates. She married Anderson because he agreed to put fifty thousand dollars in her bank account. They went arm in arm to Paris, London, New York, and then San Francisco, on whose outskirts the Lucky Swede built a monument to his bride in the form of a magnificent castle.

Big Alex McDonald went to Paris, too, and then to Rome, where he was granted an audience with the Pope and made a Knight of St. Gregory, because of his many donations to the Dawson hospital run by the Sisters of St. Anne. Then he went to London, and by the time he returned to Dawson in April 1899, he had a new bride – the twenty-year-old Margaret Chisholm, daughter of the superintendent of the Thames Water Police.

There seemed no end to McDonald's wealth. In Dawson that spring, his fifteen-mule pack train, laden with gold, was a familiar sight on the Klondike River road. One day the pack train went missing. The mules wandered about the hills for two weeks. But no one touched the gold. On one of his claims a single man was able to shovel in twenty thousand dollars in gold in a twelve-hour stretch. A single payment made by Big Alex to the Alaska Trading and Transportation Company amounted to one hundred and fifty thousand dollars.

Big Alex built his own building which he named after

himself, and he lived lavishly on its first floor. On a sideboard there was a bowl containing forty-five pounds (20 kg) of nuggets. "Help yourself to some nuggets," McDonald said to a young newspaper reporter, Alice Henderson. It was as if he was offering a box of chocolates.

"Take some of the bigger ones," he urged. When she hesitated, he said, "Oh, they mean nothing to me. Take as many as you please. There are lots more."

Back in the outside world, Swiftwater Bill, now hailed in the press as "The Klondike Prince," was publicly offering to bet seven thousand dollars on the turn of a card with anybody who cared to challenge him. He caught the eye of a Seattle widow, Mrs. Iola Beebe, and he also caught the eye of her two young daughters, Bera, aged fifteen, and Blanche, nineteen, both just out of convent school. When Mrs. Beebe's back was turned he spirited both the daughters aboard his ship which was about to steam north.

The alarmed mother boarded the boat before it left and discovered Swiftwater cowering under a lifeboat. She rescued the girls, and then decided to go north herself to seek her fortune. She and her daughters landed in Skagway, only to come upon Swiftwater lying in wait. Mrs. Beebe awoke one morning to find that he had left Dawson with the fifteen-year-old Bera. Before she could overtake them the two were married.

Swiftwater gave his bride a gift of a melon, so rare in the Klondike that it cost him forty dollars. Mrs. Beebe soon forgave him. He then managed to borrow thirty-five thousand dollars from her to finance a mining claim in the Klondike. And that was the last she saw of it.

By the end of the year Swiftwater was magnificently bankrupt, having run up bills totalling a hundred thousand dollars. He fled from Dawson with his child bride, leaving his now destitute mother-in-law to care for a four-week-old granddaughter.

Pat Galvin, the free-spending Irishman who had sunk his profits for his Bonanza claim into a transportation company, was teetering on the edge of ruin by the spring of 1899. So were many others. Galvin's first steamboat, which he designed to be the finest vessel on the river, was a complete failure; she drew so much water she couldn't cross the shallow Yukon flats and had to be abandoned. His second boat lay stranded in the ice fourteen hundred miles (2,240 km) downstream.

Galvin's financial manager, James Beatty, a fast-talking Englishman known as "Lord Jim," also helped to ruin him. Not only did he import the finest china and bed linens for Galvin's proposed chain of Yukon River hotels, but he also imported the best-looking girls to be had in San Francisco for himself. His free-spending habits caught up with him when the company's auditors found forty thousand dollars missing in his books. Beatty was arrested and charged with embezzlement, but Galvin had him released on bail and paid his way across the border into the United States.

Once on Alaskan soil, Lord Jim promptly forged a

cheque and headed for South Africa with a troop of detectives on his trail. That was billed as the longest manhunt on record. But Galvin, who had by now lost everything, didn't whimper. When he learned of Lord Jim's troubles, he merely shrugged. "He was a good fellow," he observed.

One by one the Klondike Kings toppled from their thrones. Only a few – Clarence Berry was one – kept their money. Antone Stander, having drunk part of his fortune away and given the rest to his wife, headed north again seeking another Klondike, working his passage aboard ship by peeling potatoes. He got no farther than the Alaska Panhandle and died in the Pioneers' Home in Sitka.

Dick Lowe managed to get rid of more than half a million dollars from his famous fraction. Part of it was stolen from his claim because he was too drunk to take notice of what was happening. Part of it was flung onto the bars of the saloons – as much as ten thousand dollars at a time. He had warned his friends against marrying a dance-hall girl, but in the end he married one himself.

By the turn of the century, Lowe was on his way down, trying to recoup his fortunes in other gold rushes, without success. There is a sad picture of him pawning an eight-hundred-dollar monogrammed gold watch in Victoria, B.C. There's another of him peddling water by the bucket in Fairbanks, Alaska, in 1905. He died in San Francisco in 1907.

Others met variations of the same fate. Sam Stanley of Eldorado, the bookseller's son, married a dance-hall girl and died a poor man. Jim Daugherty, who had the fanciest sled in the Klondike – the one with the built-in bar – was broke by 1902. Pat Galvin left the Klondike in 1899 bankrupt, and died shortly after of cholera in the South Seas. Frank Phiscator killed himself in a San Francisco hotel.

Even Tom Lippy, the God-fearing YMCA man who did not drink or gamble, ended his days bankrupt, even though he had taken close to two million dollars from his claim on Eldorado. After he sold out in 1903, he and his wife made a trip around the world and built the proudest home in Seattle. Lippy was generous to a fault. When obscure relatives descended upon them, he took them in and gave them jobs. He made large donations to the Methodist Church and the YMCA. He gave twenty-five thousand dollars to the Anti-Saloon League, donated the land on which the Seattle General Hospital was built, and started the drive for Seattle's first swimming pool.

Lippy became a respected citizen, hospital president, port commissioner, senior golf champion of the Pacific Northwest, but he was, alas, a bad businessman. He sank almost half a million dollars in several companies, all of which failed. Lippy was ruined, and when he died in 1931 at the age of seventy-one he had nothing to leave his wife.

Big Alex McDonald was ruined by the very thing that made him rich – his obsession with property. For several years he kept his wealth and he became the leading light in Dawson in spite of his awkwardness and lack of social presence. It was Big Alex that the townspeople chose as the key figure in a farewell celebration when the much-loved NWMP superintendent Sam Steele left the Yukon in 1899.

As a special concession, the steamboat on which the policeman was leaving was brought up the river to the front of the barracks. There, Big Alex, who had been carefully rehearsed and drilled for several days, was supposed to make a graceful farewell speech and present Steele with a poke of gold. At the last moment, the King of the Klondike lumbered forward sheepishly and thrust the gold into Steele's hand. The farewell speech went as follows: "Here, Sam – here y'are. Poke for you – goodbye."

That wasn't quite what the crowd had expected, but, in spite of it, Big Alex was chosen again to make another presentation to the wife of the Governor General of Canada when his party visited Dawson in 1900. This time the gift to Lady Minto was a golden bucket filled to the brim with curiously-shaped nuggets, with a miniature gold windlass above it.

Again Big Alex was carefully rehearsed in a speech written especially for the occasion. Alas, when the awful moment came, the King of Klondike simply reached out his great ham hands toward her ladyship and said, "Here, tak' it. It's trash."

To McDonald gold was always trash. He continued to use it to buy more land and as his claims were worked out he bought new ones farther away. He had twenty claims on one creek alone, none worth a plugged nickel. In his last year he lived by himself in a little cabin on Clearwater

Alex McDonald presents Lady Minto with a special gift.

Creek still prospecting for gold, his fortune long gone. One day a prospector came upon the cabin and found McDonald's huge form lying in front of his chopping block. He'd died of a heart attack while splitting firewood.

The liveliest Klondike sequel is provided, naturally enough, by Swiftwater Bill Gates. When the Klondike stampede ended in 1899 and gold was discovered at Nome, Alaska, Swiftwater headed for the new strike. There, he repeated his success in a mild way by taking a lay on a claim that made him four thousand dollars. He lost it all gambling.

Broke again and back in civilization, he was still the same old Swiftwater. He left his young wife and ran off with a pretty seventeen-year-old named Kitty Brandon. There was the usual wild chase from city to city with an angry mother in hot pursuit. Finally, in Chehalis, Washington, Swiftwater found a preacher to marry the pair. It was complicated, however, by the fact that (1) Swiftwater was still married to Bera Beebe, and (2) Kitty Brandon was actually his stepniece.

He solved that problem by discarding the young woman a few months after the wedding. He was scarcely a free man again when his mother-in-law, Mrs. Beebe, banged on his hotel-room door with vengeance in her eye. Swiftwater was always a fast talker. He persuaded her to pawn her diamonds so he could go back north again to recoup his fortune.

Miraculously, he did just that. He took a lay on Number

Six Cleary Creek, Fairbanks, and made seventy-five thousand dollars, only to find that he now faced two angry mothers-in-law, both of whom had followed him north.

He gave Mrs. Brandon (who was also his sister) the slip, but Mrs. Beebe was not so easy to shake off. She chased Swiftwater down the coast, and when the two reached Seattle she had him jailed for bigamy.

With the help of several bribes, Swiftwater stayed out of jail, his marital problems were untangled, both girls were properly divorced, and Swiftwater moved on. The last we hear of him is in 1935 in Peru. He died that year after he was supposedly wangling a twenty-million-acre (8 million hectares) silver-mining concession. Swiftwater Bill's story is the stuff of which Hollywood movies are made – but in this case nobody would make it because the truth was simply too far-fetched to be credible. But then the whole story of the mad rush for gold in the Klondike is scarcely believable.

Dawson, a town built to hold some twenty thousand transients, has a permanent population today of some fifteen hundred people. It still straggles along the frozen swamp on which it was built. Much of it has burned or rotted away, but recent work by Parks Canada to restore its most famous buildings has helped preserve the history of the gold rush.

The same cannot be said of most of the communities along the river, such as Fortymile, which have fallen into disrepair. The river itself, empty of steamboats, has given way to the Alaska Highway as the main thoroughfare to the gold-fields.

But men still mine placer gold along the famous old creeks. New and more sophisticated mining methods, together with the higher price of gold, have made it practical to seek and find buried treasure in the old workings. Some of these have been picked over two or three times, and are still yielding a profit.

The story of the great gold rush is very much a story of human greed and human folly, as it is also a story of high adventure and occasional heroism.

To many men, the gold was like a drug. They could not get enough of it and they had to give it away in order to get more. One of the lessons of the great stampede is that sudden riches – the pot of gold at the end of the proverbial rainbow – cannot by themselves bring happiness.

Poor men who scrambled all their lives to make a place for themselves in the world found it difficult to bear the weight of the wealth that was thrust upon them. For two or three years the Kings of the Klondike had a wonderful time spending their money. But most of them ended up as they had begun.

Few of the Klondike Kings ever achieved the immortality of a place-name. There are no references to Tom Lippy, Big Alex, or even Swiftwater Bill on the buildings that remain, and no plaques to commemorate their passing.

But William Ogilvie is remembered. An Ogilvie Bridge

crosses the Klondike River not far from Bonanza Creek. The Ogilvie Mountains can easily be seen from the hills above Dawson. And Ogilvie's original office, the oldest building in Dawson, still stands at the corner of Church and Front. Known for years as the Yukon Hotel, it has been restored by the Heritage Canada Foundation.

The story of Ogilvie and his chainman, Dick Lowe, underlines the lesson of the great stampede. Lowe, as we have seen, died broke and unhappy. Ogilvie, who never made a nickel from Klondike gold, retired to Ottawa, lived out the rest of his life with his family on a government pension, wrote a book about his experiences, and never suffered a moment's regret.

Ogilvie's legacy was greater than that of those he helped to riches. He surveyed the border between Alaska and the Yukon. He laid out much of the city of Dawson. He untangled the mess on the Bonanza claims. He became the second commissioner of the territory – a job equal to that of premier. William Ogilvie died a respected public servant. In a very real sense he was an uncrowned King of the Klondike.

Index

74

riches found in, 25
Klondike River, 11, 70-71, 72;
  Klondike valley, 9-10, 11-13

Coming Soon
The Battle of Lake Erie

Pierre Berton returns to his series on the battles of the War of 1812 in this thrilling saga of men, muskets, cannons, and sailing ships. The great naval battle on Lake Erie in the summer of 1813 was fought by fifteen battleships – nine American, six British – each one of which had been constructed of timber felled on the shores of the lake. In *The Battle of Lake Erie*, Pierre Berton vividly illustrates how two brilliant commanders fought each other to a standstill – and how one turned crushing defeat into a brilliant victory.

The Death of Tecumseh

The Shawnee chief Tecumseh was perhaps the greatest native leader in the War of 1812. Allied with the British, he was both feared and admired by his American foes. In September 1813 in what is now southwestern Ontario he fought to the death at the Battle of the Thames. To this day no one has been able to locate Tecumseh's grave, and both his death and life have become the stuff of legend.